ANNAPURNA
THE EMPIRICAL MOUNTAIN
(Fables of a Quasi-Metaphysical Civil Servant)

 Igor Barreto

Foreword by Gina Saraceni

▷ Translated from the Spanish by Rowena Hill ◁

A
ˈAlliterätion

ANNAPURNA
THE EMPIRICAL MOUNTAIN (FABLES OF A QUASI-METAPHYSICAL
CIVIL SERVANT) | IGOR BARRETO
Translated from the Spanish by Rowena Hill
First edition in English in February 2021

Design by Elisa Barrios
Cover by Andrea Martínez
Editorial Coordination by Amayra Velón

ISBN: 978-1-7378537-4-9

FLOWERS OF SNOW:
VIRTUALITY AND WRITING
IN IGOR BARRETO'S *ANNAPURNA* *

A climber is a mark on the snow

IGOR BARRETO

Annapurna is the tenth highest mountain on Earth, one of the eight-thousanders that rise in the Himalayan and Karakorom ranges in Asia, and its peaks form a massif which is one of the most dangerous in the world to climb. The first successful ascent of this mountain was made by the French team Maurice Herzog and Louis Lachenal, who reached the summit on the 3rd of June, 1950.

Annapurna is also a vanishing line that poetry opens up in language, 'a sort of athletics practiced in flight and organic defection' by 'indirect' and 'molecular roads'[1] that can lead to exhaustion, necrosis and amputation. The poet is a climber who faces the crest of language not knowing what he will find on reaching the summit, what will happen after the ascent when the rock runs out.

Annapurna. The Empirical Mountain. (Fables of a Quasi-Metaphysical Civil Servant), by the Venezuelan writer Igor Barreto, speaks of how poetry can be an experience of two opposing positions: verticality and horizontality. Through a language that transposes and traffics with knowledges and memories, the author, a river navigator and professional breeder of fighting cocks, comes and goes from the plains to the city, 'from the countryside to the elevator', from small town bars to the office and, through these movements, traces links between the things he sees and the stories he hears, between distant and present,

3

national and foreign, real and virtual, oral and visual. This action of bringing together unconnected spheres of reference requires on his part taking up an uncomfortable position within language, placing him in an area where representation goes into crisis, crashes, and the limits of sense deform and expand. From the threshold and the interval, Barreto assembles his poetics like a montage of parts and documents that unfold the history of a place - San Fernando de Apure, the river, the plains, the country - which is also the history of a way of hearing and feeling culture:

> *a poet should take the risk of placing himself within those strata, in those zones of greatest ambiguity where times meet and blend; and attempt from within the confusion and the stammering to rehearse a singing voice, expanding the possibility of a different kind of lyric[2].*

According to this fragment of *The Blind Plain*, writing means putting poetry 'beside itself', taking it out of its limits and placing it close to life and other knowledges and discourses. In this sense, Barreto's poetry belongs to a trend common to certain contemporary Latin American works, conceiving of literature as an expansive field, which in its instability and ferment infringes upon the very notion of field as a static and closed space[3] and which, besides, escapes from form and posits aesthetics as a device for making life[4].

Barreto's work, throughout its different stages[5], delivers a poetry in dialogue with materials outside or at the limit of the literary, which enter the poetic field without losing their singularity, implying a questioning and a rarefaction of the very idea of poetry. It is an oeuvre-archive, where journalistic texts coexist with oral testimony, technological references with the lexicons of the world of fighting cocks or climbers of eight-thousanders, reports with translations, geographical data with references to film which acquire a subjective dimension. From a formal point of view, different formats are also used - long poem, short poem, fragment, essay, annotation, letter, *copla*, translation - which are taken up in order to be altered and thus to point to the power of variation and contamination that life exercises as it demands an interruption of and escape from form. Even from the editorial and graphic point of view, Igor Barreto's books, published by Sociedad de Amigos del Santo Sepulcro, which he himself directs, function as small 'sarcophagi' which, as well as holding the 'essential stories' of the common people, can be considered collective tombs for affects because they list on their flaps, as memorial and homage, the 'Honorable members of the Society', founded in 1820 in San Fernando de Apure, all deceased, among whom are a few people from the family of the Argentinean writer Sergio Chefej, a friend of the poet, and even his dog Laika. A list with no period at the end so it can be infinite as the text of tradition is infinite.

From the above a first reflection on Barreto's poetry can be deduced: his tendency to expansion and contamination; his binding power and his ability to move around and connect spaces, knowledges and subjects. Poetry becomes the closest thing to life, to common life, to affect as *pathos* and crisis. The wreck of a steamer, the murder of a horse, the flooding of the plains or a cock fight are the raw material of his poetry; the 'black zone of the concrete' where a man dies because a caiman swallows him or a climber does not survive an avalanche; at the threshold of indetermination where life exceeds and disarticulates itself, the poet 'rehearses' 'a different kind of lyric' which conveys the emotions of a particular community.

Annapurna. The Empirical Mountain (Fables of a Quasi-Metaphysical Civil Servant) is one of his most political books - together with *El Duelo* (Mourning) and *Carreteras nocturnas* (Night Roads), both 2010 - and expresses Barreto's unease and disagreement with what he calls 'the accursed circumstance of the present everywhere'. Starting from references to particular experiences and multiple knowledges and discourses, he conveys the implications and consequences of the present Venezuelan political situation for the life of the people. For this purpose he uses the antipodes as a figure based on the comparison and opposition between spaces and events which can show the disaccord between the poet and reality. And *Annapurna* is the place where this figure acquires an extreme forcefulness.

The traveler of the plains, navigator of the River Apure, breeder of cocks and bettor on their fights, is now a civil servant in the Ministry of People's Power for Culture, who spends his days shut up in an office where Monday is like a 'coffee stain' and Friday is the same, and who seeks to escape through the computer which offers him the chance to attempt one of the most daring enterprises that a human being can face: climbing Annapurna. The civil servant has 'nothing to do/ unless to travel by Google Earth', because the desolate routine of administrative reports and papers casts him into the most radical boredom and leads him to undertake a virtual journey through remote regions: 'I fled to 10,000, 20,000 meters altitude/ and strayed toward the stagnant desert of Pakistan (...) And if the salary runs away by a filthy ditch/ I swear I will never descend from Annapurna:/ - to the hills of Towertorrible/ tedium -'.

I want to emphasize that the first edition of *Annapurna* includes some images that I am not going to analyze but over which I will pause briefly, because they provide additional evidence of the gestures of appropriation, intervention and contamination in Barreto's poetry. The book is square and opens and closes with a black page which, together with the white of the cover, alludes to the death of the mountain. This is followed by: a digital photo of the aerial view of the territory of Annapurna, a negative of the mountain and a black page with the outline of a white triangle, on the back of which is a calligram, also triangular, dedicated to Carlos Drummond de Andrade; both images seem to simplify the image of the mountain and turn it into a geometrical figure. At the end of the book, beside the penultimate poem entitled 'Final declaration of a civil servant', there is a negative of the Torres del Silencio, the site of the office that functions as an antipodes- image of Annapurna. Finally, the book closes with an appendix entitled 'Photographs of a civil servant': a photo in color of the office and the dead archive of the museum which shows, together with the image of the author, that of the designers of the book, the corrector, Yolanda Pantin to whom the book is dedicated, Alfredo Herrera (a poet and friend of the author), the ghost of his dog Laika flying, and two images of a computer screen with Barreto's hands in the foreground 'framing' the photos of the two climbers who were the first to reach the summit of Annapurna.

In this book, Barreto performs one of the most daring experiments of his aesthetic project, constructing what I want to call a *geopoetic machine*, a verbal device capable both of connecting distant, real and virtual geographical spaces, which thus become co-existent and simultaneous, and of infecting and linking modes of speech, terms and words which are at the same time specific and not specific to a particular knowledge because they have been carried to the limit of their capacity to signify. The athletic power of this machine draws together the office in the ministry and a block of ice, an administrator and a climber, a climber and a poet, bureaucracy and trekking, Buddha and the acting head of the dead archive, the crest of Annapurna and a tropical sunset, and even succeeds in making Annapurna 'a piece in a Lego/ bought at the American Toy Store/ in Colinas de Bello Monte, Caracas, Venezuela'.

The civil servant-poet-climber is in his office in Caracas, which is at the same time the mountain, 'the shoulder of the planet,/ its back'. This linking brought about by the geopoetic machine is the result of the appropriation of lexicons belonging to mountain climbing, geography, cinema, medicine, Buddhism, bureaucracy, all necessary to stage one of the borderline experiences of the human body, which is also an experience of the limits of language: to ascend the mountain, like the climbers, it has to make a huge effort and runs out of oxygen. 'Putting on the outfit is an act of depersonalization', says a line

7

in the book. Besides drawing attention to the alteration in the appearance and faces of the climbers, this refers to the rarefying of language itself, which has to 'outfit' itself with other vocabularies, other word 'harnesses', to be able to face the highest rock in the world. This practice of contaminating poetry with specialized terminologies is a core aspect of Barreto's poetry. As he expresses it in *The Blind Plain*:

> *I would like special attention to be paid to proper names, a lexicon of seasoned resonances and recondite toponimies. What's involved is a verbal archaeology. Although those words have lost their meaning for many, they go on resounding in the hidden ear of the language: they will bejewel the verse, giving it atmosphere and sonority*[6].

The poetry that ascends Annapurna from a ministry office becomes a 'language minting machine', where the residues of languages settle and accumulate, as on the mountain the waste that the climbers leave on the snows settles and accumulates: 'remains of sleeping tents, cellophane biscuit packets, and also corpses'.

In Barreto beauty is always the place of disaster and of the greatest vulnerability, as if there was an intimate defect in the beautiful related with its durability. In these mineral and white landscapes which surprise with their grandeur and their radical otherness, death reigns. Maurice Herzog, Louis Lachenal, Iñaki, David Sharp, Scott Fischer, Chantal Mauduit, Laila Rosemberg, Amy Cubert, Leo Feltrinelli, Juan Ignacio Apellániz, Narayan Sherestra, Atxo, little Alessio, great climbers who summited or died in the intent, form a community of desire: their greatest aspiration is to reach the most difficult summit in the world, and after succeeding to descend and dream of a fresh ascent. 'How can a rock inspire honor/ and call to the spirit?' the poem asks these men who seek a 'way of elevation' and fight against every kind of physical, geographical or atmospheric adversity that could take their lives. 'We are minute scraps of flint/ descending by a white sea'... 'A man is nothing but no one/ tied to a rope'.

In the same way as the Apure river in Igor Barreto's previous books is the tomb of the people who drowned and disappeared in its waters, Annapurna is the tomb of the climbers whose ambition was to bring 'the cardiogram of the heart' to 'breaking point', and who died because of an avalanche, an edema, a necrosis, a septicemia, a gangrene, or because they fell into the void 'like a robin fledgling/ from an unsafe nest'. Beneath the glacier the same shouts echo as are heard under the waters of the river; before it was the sailors, now it is the climbers, and poetry reaches where neither rescue teams nor helicopters can reach: 'I write the ridge, the flowers of ice dropping,/ the force of gravity/ that leads me to the body that will not be found'.

The poet who belongs to this reckless community is at the same time a civil servant who tries daily to defend himself against a routine that diminishes and humiliates him, as he looks at 'a ministry building/ like a mountain in Nepal'. Like a climber, every day he ascends his concrete mountain in the elevator to the summit of his office where, as on the eight-thousanders, it is an effort to breathe. But, in contrast to the mountain which grants fame and satisfaction to those who climb it, the one in the Torres del Silencio in Caracas is an 'empirical mountain' which rises over the disaster of an inoperative system and is threatened by a death zone which shows daily the void of which it consists. The civil servant works in the abyss. 'Nothing to do' is the work he faces every day. 'I lead my stark life/ in this office/ where the changeless feature/ is a green/ taro vine'. From tedium and despair he goes in and out of the image that the computer offers him, breaking the barrier of temporality and spatiality. But his aspiration to ascend the mountain and reach the summit is nothing more than the experience of the horizontality of a sequence of photographs unfolding. 'There is no greater degradation of experience, there is no greater desolation', Barreto says. 'The civil servant believes he escapes from his exile by consuming a protocol created by a transnational company and through the illusory virtual reality of the technology industry'.

In this sense *Annapurna* shows how the way of escape that Google Earth provides for moving round the world is only the realization of the impossibility of an encounter with a reality not mediated by the ever more sophisticated and hyperreal representation of the media. On his digital journey, the civil servant touches the shoulder of the planet, but 'Annapurna/ is nothing but an image on a/ computer screen./ But how it hurts!' This exclamation reveals the pain caused by the horizontality without accidents of the digital image and the absence of organic evidence in the photos, which in their turn are also the horizontality of the wall of the present where no satisfaction is possible. The poem is hurt by its athletic fitness which lets it ascend 'chunks of snow ice' and listen to the 'crash' of avalanches, because in reality what its hands are touching is 'administrative documents' and its eyes are frozen on the computer screen with its 'chromatism' and its 'well calibrated shine'. 'Nothing to do, nothing to do/ unless to travel with Google Earth' is what the poem repeats and what the poet-civil servant does every day to defend himself from the miserable salary and from life itself which is collapsing like the 'flowers of ice' that drop from the most difficult mountain on Earth.

Gina Saraceni

NOTES

* This text was published with slight changes and under a different title in *Revista de Literatura Hispánica* n.° 87-88, *primavera-otoño*, 2018, pp. 272-282

1 Gilles Deleuze. *Crítica y clínica*. Barcelona: Editorial Anagrama, 1996, p. 6.
2 Igor Barreto. *The Blind Plain. Portland:Tavern Books, 2017, p.223.*

3   Florencia Garramuño. *Mundos en común. Ensayos sobre la inespecifidad en el arte*. Buenos Aires: Fondo de Cultura Económica, 2015, p. 43.

4   Fermín Rodríguez. "Latin American Psycho". In *Entre el humo y la niebla. Guerra y cultura en América Latina*, pp. 291-314. Pittsburgh: Instituto Internacional de Literatura Latinoamericana, Universidad de Pittsburgh, 2016.

5   *¿Y si el amor no llega?* (1983), *Soy el muchacho más hermoso de esta ciudad* (1989), *Crónicas llanas* (1989), *Tierranegra* (1993), *Carama* (2000), *Soul of Apure* (2006), *El llano ciego* (2006), *El duelo* (2010), *Carreteras nocturnas* (2010), *Annapurna* (2012).

6   Igor Barreto. *The Blind Plain*. Portland:Tavern Books, 2017, p.277.

ANNAPURNA
THE EMPIRICAL MOUNTAIN
(Fables of a Quasi-Metaphysical Civil Servant)

to Yolanda P.
office partner

As the mountain swept me up in its flight,
I suddenly saw open before me,
on the other space,
the golden door of Memory,
the way out of the labyrinth.
THE POEM OF THE ARCANA O.W. LUBICZ MILOSZ

I sing a song
for a white
temple.
TIBETAN POPULAR SONG

Así que la montaña me hubo arrastrado en su vuelo,
vi de pronto abrirse ante mí,
sobre el otro espacio,
la puerta de oro de la Memoria,
la salida del laberinto.
EL POEMA DE LOS ARCANOS O.W. LUBICZ MILOSZ

Canto una canción
para un templo
blanco.
ANÓNIMO POPULAR DEL TÍBET

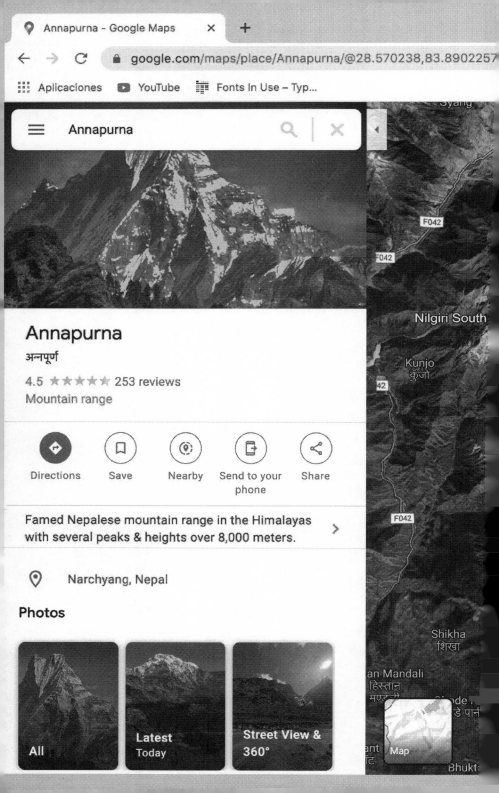

!3m1!1e3!4m5!3m4!1s0x39be1c44051f84f7:0x941cbed25f0b39fb!8m2!...

A
hora soy
un funcionario
público. Y el Annapurna
es apenas una imagen en la
pantalla del ordenador. ¡Pero cómo duele!

(CALIGRAMA PARA CARLOS DRUMMOND DE ANDRADE)

I
am now
a civil servant.
And Annapurna
is nothing but an image on a
computer screen. But how it hurts!

(Calligram for Carlos Drummond de Andrade)

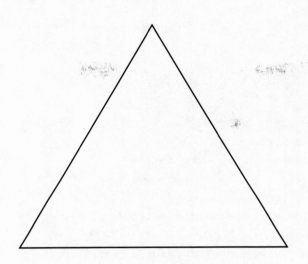

Ícaro-Escalador
(En arriesgado viaje virtual)

Desde aquí puedo ver la crisálida del Annapurna
gobernando la zona de muerte de los ochomiles.
Digo, que ahora vuelo como cualquier otro aro niquelado
de la esfera terrestre,
a 10.000 kilómetros de altura, mientras
fijo mi vista en la montaña que es una epifanía
de la Diosa de las cosechas.
Ella siega la cabeza de los escaladores, la corona de trigo
con las semillas germinadas
y las arroja al final de laderas y despeñaderos.
Una montaña es un emblema del reino mineral
—eso me han dicho—
pero la soledad y el vacío del espacio a esta altura
ha reinventado la tristeza por la ausencia de lo orgánico.
Creo que se trata de un pattern síquico.
Deseo ver a la tierra como una bellota,
como un fruto empujado desde su interior por una semilla
que es la cresta himalayística del Annapurna,
bordeando imaginarios lugares del Tíbet y Nepal.

Icarus-Climber
(On a hazardous virtual journey)

From here I can see the chrysalis of Annapurna
ruling over the Death Zone of the eight-thousanders.
I say, now I am flying like any other nickel-plated ring
of the terrestrial sphere,
at 10,000 kilometers altitude, while
I keep my eyes on the mountain which is an epiphany
of the Goddess of harvests.
She shears off the heads of the climbers, the crowns of corn
with the sprouted grains
and flings them to the bottom of slopes and precipices.
A mountain is an emblem of the mineral kingdom
– so I've been told –
but the desolation and blankness of space at this altitude
have redefined sadness at the absence of anything organic.
I think it's a case of a psychic pattern.
I want to see the earth as an acorn,
as a fruit pushed from inside by a seed
which is the Himalayan crest of Annapurna,
bordering imaginary places in Tibet and Nepal.

Destino

La montaña sólo espejea la oscuridad cósmica

      mientras floto

en el área de rotación

      antes de la noche:

[Desde aquí puedo ver el orbe rodador   de los cometas,
su ánima dispersiva.
Veo las estrellas dividiéndose en un acto puro de replicación.
Vi una lluvia de aerolitos que manchaban de violetas
y magentas - la bóveda].

Hay quienes hablan y sueñan con el Annapurna,
pero muy pocos conocen
      la montaña empírica.

Será preciso que entremos en el centro de una tensión antigua,/ guiados por la fuerza de gravedad, y sólo con palabras:/ como si estas fuesen alfiles en un tablero.

26

Destination

The mountain only mirrors the cosmic darkness

      while I float

on the current of rotation

      before nightfall:

[From here I can see the rolling orbs   of the comets,
their will to disperse.
I see the stars splitting in a pure act of replication.
I saw a shower of aerolites that stained the vault
with violets and magentas.]

There are people who talk and dream of Annapurna,
but very few know
        the empirical mountain.

We will be required to enter the center of an ancient tension,/ guided by the
force of gravity, and only with words:/ as if they were bishops on a chessboard.

27

Ciclos

Antes de llegar la luz del día a la Piazza del Duomo
en Florencia
o a la retícula de un rascacielos
en el Financial Center de Shanghai,
se ilumina la cresta del Annapurna
y el sol calibra su cromaticidad con la montaña:
de un color neutro
a otro más saturado: del blanco al rojo. Simplemente amanece
entre juegos ambiguos.
Perfilo el papel para la copia de mis sueños himalayísticos.
Escribo la arista, las flores del hielo que se desploman,
la fuerza de gravedad
que me conduce al cuerpo que no será encontrado.

Cycles

Before the light of day reaches Piazza Duomo
in Florence
or the grid of a skyscraper
in the Financial Center of Shanghai,
the crest of Annapurna lights up
and the sun calibrates its chromaticity by the mountain:
from a neutral color
to one more saturated: from white to red. Simply, it dawns
between ambiguous games.
I trim the paper for the copy of my Himalayan dreams.
I write the ridge, the flowers of ice dropping,
the force of gravity
that leads me to the body that will not be found.

Haciendo foco

Al buscar por primera vez la palabra «Annapurna» en Internet
—tras los cristales aspaventosos de la oficina—
apareció la imagen de un restaurant
de comida rápida vegetariana:
y no La avellana gris del Nepal.
Esta montaña es el hombro del planeta,
y su espalda.
Hay rasgaduras asestadas por la hoja de una navaja
de tamaño impensable.
Al mirar oblicuamente por riscos y abismos
se desata otra perspectiva:
acontecimientos transreales, reflejos retroactivos
y cuadros bufos
de nuestra ascensión al cielo.

Focusing

The first time I looked for the word "Annapurna" on the Internet
– behind the ghostly window panes of the office –
the picture of a fast food vegetarian
restaurant appeared
and not the gray hazelnut of the Nepal.
This mountain is the shoulder of the planet,
its back.
There are gashes inflicted by the blade of a knife
of unthinkable size.
Looking sideways along bluffs and chasms
a different perspective erupts:
transreal happenings, retroactive reflections
and farcical pictures
of our ascent to the sky.

Un peine de hueso

Muchos han muerto con los pulmones llenos de agua
en una caverna de hielo azul, con palabras que no hacían falta.
Es absurdo: ¿cómo una roca puede inspirar honor
y llamar al espíritu?
Aquí el viento sopla a 60° sub-cero, y todavía hay escaladores
que se entrampan
concentrándose en lo que ya no tienen.
Algo como esto les ocurrió a Scott Fischer, y a Chantal Mauduit
que escuchaba a Haendel
cuando probó la ceguera de la montaña
al descender del techo de los ochomiles
—como las puntas más altas de un peine de hueso—.
En definitiva,
el escalador es una marca sobre la nieve.
Pensemos en algo parecido a un punto y coma:
el punto fue el escalador, y la coma, la cordada que sostenía
a Fischer y a Chantal Mauduit.
Una de las cuatro manos
de una Diosa pálida e hindú
al parecer trazó estos signos
que el viento hizo vibrar con furia y miedos.

A comb of bone

Many have died with their lungs full of water,
in a cavern of blue ice, with unnecessary words.
It's absurd: how can a rock inspire honor
and call to the spirit?
Here the wind blows at 60 degrees below zero, and still there are
      climbers
who delude themselves
concentrating on what they no longer have.
Something like this happened to Scott Fischer, and to Chantal
      Mauduit,
who was listening to Handel
when she tasted mountain blindness
on descending from the roof of the eight-thousanders
– like the highest points in a comb of bone.
In the end,
a climber is a mark on the snow.
Think of something like a semicolon:
the dot was the climber, and the comma the rope holding
Fischer and Chantal Mauduit.
One of the four hands
of a pale Hindu Goddess
drew it seems these signs
that shook in the wind with rage and fear.

Lección del auriga

Un día, Buddha salió con su carruaje alado
conducido por un auriga,
era la primera vez que volaban
sobre los riscos altos de la montaña
y en el trayecto de ese viaje encontró a un escalador coreano,
a los que suelen acusar corrientemente de suicidas.
El escalador había muerto hace por lo menos cinco años
y aún conservaba sus brazos rodeando el pecho
como un último gesto antes de la congelación.
Durante largo tiempo sus pertenencias permanecieron intactas:
la cámara fotográfica, el abrigo de plástico anaranjado y gris,
el piolín que colgaba de su mano izquierda,
y en sus pies los dos crampones -sorpresivamente nuevos-.
Dolido por aquella visión, preguntó Buddha al auriga:
¿Qué ha hecho, buen auriga, este hombre?
—Alteza, esto es lo que se conoce como un escalador.
—¿Y qué es, buen auriga,
lo que se conoce como un escalador?
—Un escalador, alteza, significa un ser con demasiada ambición
y al que no le resta mucho por vivir.

Lesson of the charioteer

One day, Buddha went out in his winged carriage
driven by a charioteer;
it was the first time they were flying
over the high crags of the mountain,
and on that trip he met one of those Korean climbers
that lately have been accused of being suicidal.
The climber had been dead for at least five years
and still had his arms around his chest,
his last gesture before freezing.
For a long time his belongings had remained intact:
his camera, his orange and gray plastic jacket,
the ice hammer hanging from his left hand
and on his feet the two – surprisingly new – crampons.
Saddened by that sight, Buddha asked the charioteer:
– *What has he done, good charioteer, this man?*
– *Highness, this is what is known as a climber.*
– *And what is it, good charioteer,*
that is known as a climber?
– *A climber, Highness, means a person with too much ambition*
who doesn't have much longer to live.

David Sharp

Cómo olvidar a David Sharp en su agonía por falta de oxígeno.
Derretí agua con la boca y se la di. Era la faz del edema.
Por momentos me pareció escuchar su voz:
— Sal a mi encuentro y ábreme huella.
También imaginé que había una pared
que daba paso a una arista
y luego, otra pared y otra arista...
Salí de aquella carpa —abrumado— pensando
que en estas montañas
cuando ocurre una avalancha:
no hay demonio, ni disnea, y el escalador
queda envuelto en la formación de la pureza.
Y si llegas a encontrarte muy cerca de la cumbre,
digamos a 100 m:
o el viento (el Dios Vaiu o Anila) te arroja y caes al Nepal,
o si prefieres desmembrado al Tíbet:
cantando sobre farallones verticales y altas terrazas.
Tu sangre podría teñir los bosques de coníferas de Kashmir.
De pronto las rocas han comenzado a moverse
muy próximas al helicóptero de salvamento
y descendió un sherpa que habló en un inglés nepalí.
Había pequeños remolinos de nieve que giraban sobre el suelo
y las huellas donde hace apenas dos días
encontramos enterrada una lámpara de queroseno.
Aquellos eran signos terribles
en un ambiente de mucha tranquilidad.
Yo miré las cambiantes manchas de luz
y los efectos iridiscentes del glaciar.
No podía hacer nada, nada que hacer.
El sentido común animal había regresado
al cuerpo de David Sharp.

David Sharp

How can I forget David Sharp in his death throes from lack of oxygen.
I melted water in my mouth and gave it to him. He was the face
    of edema.
At moments I thought I heard his voice:
— *Come out to meet me and clear me a trail.*
I also imagined there was a wall
which led to a ridge
and then, another wall and another ridge...
I left that tent — afflicted — thinking
that in these mountains
when an avalanche occurs
there is no demon, nor dyspnea, and the climber
is shrouded in a formation of purity.
And if you happen to be very near the summit,
say 100 meters away,
and the wind (the god Vayu or Anil) tosses you, you fall in Nepal,
or if you prefer dismembered in Tibet,
singing on vertical outcrops and high terraces.
Your blood might dye the pine forests of Kashmir.
Suddenly the rocks began to move
very close to the rescue helicopter
and a sherpa got down speaking Nepali English.
There were little eddies of snow whirling on the ground
and the footprints where just two days ago
we found a kerosene lamp buried.
Those were terrible signs
in a very tranquil setting.
I watched the changing patches of light
and the iridescent effects on the glacier.
Nothing I could do, nothing to be done.
Animal common sense had returned
to the body of David Sharp.

Pues... ahora,
ya estaba seguro
de que podría llegar la Sexta Flota
y nadie lo sacaría vivo de esa carpa.

So... now,
he was already sure
that the Sixth Fleet could come
and no one would bring him alive out of that tent.

Necrosis

¡Oh, necrosis!, perfecta asesina.
Al principio eras sólo una mancha
en el dorso del pulgar del pie izquierdo,
allí donde la carne forma estrías circulares.
El dedo se inclinó un poco
como si lo tensara un hilo invisible de araña.
La mención no está demás; filamentos helados
lo inmovilizaron deteniendo los mínimos caudales de sangre.
Herví agua en una escudilla de aluminio para calentar los pies
y en la ebullición se apareció la Diosa segadora
con sus cuatro manos
ofreciéndome una cosecha de té rojo y esencias.
—Lasciatemi morire!, Lasciatemi morire!
Entonces, el pulgar se fue acanalando y dio paso
a pequeñas supuraciones.
Afuera, la ventisca, agitaba una luz.

CODA
Primera estrofa de una vieja canción nepalí:

La montaña está excitada.
La montaña siente miedo.
La montaña es sólo sueño.

Necrosis

Oh, necrosis! perfect assassin.
To start with you were just a stain
on the back of my left big toe
where the creases in the flesh form circles.
The toe bent a little
as if pulled tight by an invisible spider's thread.
The reference is not out of place; frozen filaments
immobilized it stopping the slightest flow of blood.
I boiled water in an aluminum bowl to warm my feet
and in the seething the reaper Goddess appeared
with her four hands
offering me a harvest of red tea and spices.
–*Lasciatemi morire! Lasciatemi morire!*
Then, cracks opened in the toe and emitted
a small ooze of pus.
Outside, the blizzard, a light waving.

CODA
First verse of an old Nepali song:

The mountain is aroused.
The mountain feels afraid.
The mountain is only a dream.

Avalanchas

No cesa el crash, crash, de las avalanchas
y el choque contra la pared que forma parte del glaciar.
Hay quienes hablan de una sinfonía de sonidos: —todos reímos—.
Habíamos hecho un círculo para un porqué, o para qué.
Trozos de hielo-nieve, trozos de miedo
se desprenden sobre las tiendas de campaña,
arrugadas o tensadas, a punto
del desgarramiento.
La tormenta nos atrapó como si fuéramos sus rehenes.
La luz de una lámpara de butano salía al encuentro del hombre
de las orejas rojas: —¡Oh, viejo zorro de las nieves!
que tomas somníferos cuando la altura te espanta el sueño.
Los escaladores profesamos una vía de elevación,
donde el Ser se oculta
en un abrigo de fibra de vidrio.

Avalanches

The crash, crash of the avalanches never ceases
and the smashing against the wall which forms part of the
    glacier.
There are people who speak of a symphony of sounds: – we all
    laughed.
We had made a circle for a why, or a what for.
Chunks of snow ice, chunks of fear
break off above the tents
wrinkled or taut, about
to rip open.
The storm trapped us as if we were its hostages.
The light of a butane lamp went out to meet the man
with red ears: Oh, old fox of the snows!
you take sleeping pills when the altitude keeps you awake.
We climbers profess a way of elevation
where Being is concealed
in a fiberglass jacket.

Ángulo en picada

En el espolón norte del Annapurna,
hay un glaciar en forma de hoz.
Y en caída libre, vemos la loza de un cañón entre rocas
—bajo una luz meramente terrenal—
y algunas casas con sus huertos: que son como la borra del té
que se acumula inerme.

La creación es muda, como el destello de un ordenador de buena marca.

Swooping view

On the north spur of Annapurna
there's a sickle-shaped glacier.
And in free fall we see the slate of a canyon between rocks
— in a merely terrestrial light —
and some houses with their kitchen gardens: which are like tea leaves
in a defenseless pile.

Creation is mute, like the glitter of a computer of a good brand.

Descenso

El descenso será difícil, la oralidad se torna atropellada,
hay dificultad para repetir las mismas palabras.
Pasan las horas y no tenemos coraje ni consolación; se lucha
contra la gangrena y la septicemia.
Somos minúsculos trozos de pedernal
que descienden por un mar blanco:
la ante-tierra blanca.
La siempre esperada, la esperanza máxima.
En el campamento N° 6 soñé con Islandia: su lago azul
perfectamente circular.
Nos hundíamos como paladas en la nieve.
Antes de partir, pintamos la tienda de campaña
con anilina roja
para ser vistos fácilmente (pero no resultó).
Y luego llegaron las avalanchas
como un envión de cosas desechas.

CODA
Haiku nepalí:

Hay una ardura en la noche
y el resplandor fluorescente
de un túmulo de nieve.

Descent

The descent will be arduous, speech becomes garbled,
it's difficult to repeat the same words.
The hours pass and we have neither courage nor consolation; we
fight
against gangrene and septicemia.
We are minute scraps of flint
descending on a white sea:
the white pre-earth.
The constant hope, the highest hope.
In camp No.6 I dreamed of Iceland: its perfectly round
blue lake.
We were sinking like spades in the snow.
Before we set out, we colored the tent
with red aniline dye
to be seen easily (but it didn't work).
And then the avalanches arrived
like a barrage of spoiled things.

CODA
Nepali haiku:

*There's a torment in the night
and the fluorescent shine
of a mound of snow.*

Diagnóstico

Según la opinión del Dr. Klein:
los intensos recuerdos familiares: la fotografía de una perra Collie frente
a la barda recién bruñida de pintura blanca, la piscina inflable
rebosando el agua sobre la grama y algunas palabras en italiano, la
bandeja con galletas de avena, el carmín de la pintura de sus labios:
todo ello mantuvo cierta cantidad de glucosa, y una calidez en esa parte
del cerebro donde radica la voluntad.
Eso lo salvó.

CODA
Antigua sentencia:

… Uno es apenas nadie
atado a una cuerda.

Diagnosis

In the opinion of Dr. Klein:
intense family memories: the photograph of a collie dog in front
of a fence recently painted a glossy white, the inflatable
swimming pool spilling water on to the grass and a few words
in Italian, the tray with oatmeal biscuits, the carmine of her
lipstick: all that kept a certain quantity of glucose, and a warmth,
in that part of the brain where the will resides.
That saved him.

CODA
Ancient precept:

*... A man is hardly no one
tied to a rope.*

Iñaki

La esperanza fue lo que guio a Iñaki a ninguna parte.
Sacó el pañuelo para decir adiós al espolón de la cumbre,
a las cornisas de hielo que le parecían simples regrets éternels.
Ahora bien: —¿Cómo tirar la toalla a 7.400 m de altura,
sobre el entarimado nuboso de la montaña?
Fueron secuencias oníricas: el escarabajo de la muerte
daba vueltas en el aire premórbido y agramatical.
La dexametasona puede salvarte del edema, si la tienes, si no,
escucharás la trompeta de los monjes
trajeados en púrpura y amarillo.

CODA
Frase póstuma:

El coraje sin miedo es una estupidez.

Iñaki

Hope was what led Iñaki to nowhere.
He took out his handkerchief to say goodbye to the summit
spur,
to the cornices of ice that looked to him like simple *regrets
éternels*.
That said, how to throw in the towel at 7,400 meters altitude,
on the cloudy platform of the mountain?
Oneiric sequences: the scarab of death
flew round and round in the pre-morbid and agrammatical air.
Dexametasone can save you from edema, if you have it; if not
you will hear the trumpets of the monks
robed in purple and yellow.

CODA
Posthumous sentence:

Courage without fear is stupidity.

Primeros reflejos

Regresabas del congelamiento y éramos felices porque ya no estarías en el virtual cemetery de YouTube. En este presente sin memoria se despierta tu máquina de acuñación lingüística. Rodaste por el lomo plateado de la anticumbre hasta el borde de un farallón vertical. Iniciamos el descenso sobre la punta de nuestros crampones para alcanzar aquella terraza. El aire polvoso no dejaba respirar. Ahora, después de dos días, nuestros rostros están tan abotagados, y oímos tus primeros reflejos:

Ser lo que habré sido.
Recordar lo que hablaré.
Sufrir lo dolido.
Escribir lo que no escribo.
Háblame sin conocer.
El tiempo pasado será nunca.

First reflections

You were coming back from freezing and we were happy
because you would no longer be in the virtual cemetery of
YouTube. In this present time without memory your language
minting machine wakes. You rolled down the silver slope of the
false summit to the brink of a vertical cliff. We started the
descent on the tips of our crampons to reach that terrace. The
powdery air made it hard to breathe. Now, two days later, our
faces are very bloated, and we listen to your first reflections:

To be what I will have been.
To remember what I will speak.
To suffer what hurt.
To write what I don't write.
Speak to me without knowing.
Past time will never be.

Declaración al pie de una montaña

Luego de que bebimos un té rojo, Xiomi hizo muecas a la cámara de video y recitó esta declaración tan docta: Ascender el Annapurna es casi como subir al último piso de un edificio nepalí en Katmandú o Biratnagar. Donde los sucesivos inquilinos como estilos arquitectónicos se asoman a distinta altura. Franceses e italianos, alemanes e ingleses, se disputaron la cima y fueron dejando sus deyecciones: restos de carpas para dormir, bolsas de papel celofán para galletas, y también cadáveres. Todo, como las placas de residuos superpuestos de una roca. Así ascendimos, bajo la violencia del sol.

CODA
Sentencia nepalí:

Ahorra tu aliento.

Statement at the foot of a mountain

After we drank red tea, Xiomi made faces at the video camera
and delivered this very erudite statement: Ascending
Annapurna is almost like climbing to the top floor of a Nepali
building in Kathmandu or Biratnagar. Where successive
lodgers like architectural styles look out at different heights.
French and Italian, German and English, they disputed the
summit and went on leaving their waste: remains of sleeping
tents, cellophane biscuit packets, and also corpses. Everything,
like the overlapping layers of residues in a rock. And so we
ascended, under the violence of the sun.

CODA
Nepali precept:

Save your breath.

Vía de elevación

Colocarse el equipo es un acto despersonalizante.
En la medida en que el ascenso se realiza
abandona tu nombre:
la visión de una carretera recta,
aquellos galpones industriales como nidos de orugas,
la nieve sacrificada contra el parabrisas
 o el video de la sala del apartamento
de Salvador Dos Santos
con hortensias azulpúrpuras.
Siempre el alma resueña estos lugares.
Aparecerán rostros no conocidos y situaciones fantasmáticas.
Cuando asciendes tu imaginación debe estar apagada.
Si lo haces en solitario
puedes lograr una cierta actividad sexual con la montaña.
En ese instante, el cardiograma del corazón estará
a punto de romperse
y tus orejas serán como las manzanas de Marpha.
Cuídate: y mantendrás a raya la posible sorpresa.

CODA
Antigua canción nepalí:

Roca seca-roca helada.
Soleado viento del norte,
o abrumador viento del oeste.

The way of elevation

Putting on the outfit is an act of depersonalization.
As the ascent proceeds
abandon your name:
the vision of a straight road,
those industrial sheds like caterpillar nests,
the snow sacrificed against the windshield
or the video of the lounge in the apartment
in Salvador Dos Santos
with bluish purple hydrangeas.
The soul dreams these places over and over.
Unfamiliar faces and phantasmagoric situations will appear.
While you ascend your imagination must be turned off.
If you go by yourself
you may achieve a certain sexual activity with the mountain.
At that instant, the cardiogram of the heart will be
at breaking point
and your ears will be like the apples of Marpha.
Take care, and you will ward off the possible surprise.

CODA
Old Nepali song:

Dry rock - frozen rock.
Sunny north wind,
or overpowering west wind.

A, B, C

a) A Juan Ignacio Apellániz lo sorprendió una tormenta cuando descendía del K2. Fingía despreocupación pero estaba realmente interesado en salvarse. Al morir pronunció dos palabras: ¡Demasiado espacio!

b) A Narayan Sherestra lo mató una avalancha en el Everest: abrumado y con miedo tembloroso. Sólo podría decir que tuvo la muerte que le corresponde.

c) Atxo murió de agotamiento. Levantaba la vista y sonreía a lo inmóvil. Dejó escrito: Yo provengo de ciudades muertas.

Los tres se durmieron en medio de un tráfico ilimitado de llamadas. La noticia nos ha dejado helados.

CODA
Pensamiento póstumo:

Estas montañas son catedrales donde practicar nuestra religión.
                                                    Anatoli Boukreev

A, B, C

a) Juan Ignacio Apellániz was overtaken by a storm while descending from K2. He pretended to be unconcerned but he was really interested in saving himself. As he died he pronounced three words: Too much space!
b) Narayan Sherestra was killed by an avalanche on Everest, overwhelmed and shaking with fear. He could only have said it was the proper death for him.
c) Atxo died of exhaustion. He raised his eyes and smiled at immobility. He left a note: I come from dead cities.

All three fell asleep in the midst of an unlimited traffic of phone calls. The news has left us frozen.

CODA
Posthumous thought:

These mountains are cathedrals where we practice our religion.
                                                    Anatoli Boukreev

Suspiros en la noche solitaria

Escalador 1. —Es nuestro segundo día camino al cielo y acampamos en la gruta de un glacial: un hueco bajo una escalera: [La cabeza de la luna / se ocultó tras dos picachos]. Añoraba un blues de Bessi Smith, pero tuve que conformarme con la hazaña del escalador amante de la música de Juan Sebastián Bach. Mientras habla y habla, la misma partitura de una historia, flotamos como boyas en lo negro. En fin, escuchemos:

Escalador 2. —(...) hacía diminuendos, y aun en la distensión aparentaba un esfuerzo enorme. No quería renunciar a la cumbre. La idea era ascender tanto como pudiera resistir la línea melódica. Me refugiaba en registros agudos. Mi rango tonal se expandía y se contraía: escalando literalmente cada nota.

Escalador 1. —Zzz...

Sighs in the lonely night

Climber 1. – It's our second day on the way to the sky and we're camped in a cave in a glacier: a hole under a ladder. *[The moon's head / hid between two peaks.]* I was longing for a blues by Bessie Smith, but I had to settle for the exploits of the climber who loved the music of Johann Sebastian Bach. While he talks and talks, always the same score of a story, we float like buoys in the blackness. Anyway, let's listen:

Climber 2. – (...) I was doing diminuendos and even as the tension eased it seemed to be a huge effort. I didn't want to give up the summit. The idea was to ascend as far as the melodic line could hold out. I took refuge in high registers.
My tonal range expanded and contracted: literally scaling every note.

Climber 1. – Zzz...

Sinfé

Los sherpas han traído bombonas de oxígeno
con verdadero celo
y se apoyan en la roca y en su respiración incesante:
—¡Sherpa, busca a nuestro amigo y te daré 100 dólares!
Ellos hablan de un pájaro de extremo mimetismo.
Un pájaro que dicen, se llama, El Sinfé:
color filo dentado de risco.
Y sólo canta al fondo de la gruta del oído
cuando el aire se cristaliza
en ese azul -insustancial-.
La palabra de un sherpa, a quien se le ha mutilado
por congelamiento,
los dedos de manos y pies,
siempre ha sido muy fiable.

Nohope

The sherpas have brought oxygen cylinders
with genuine zeal
and they lean on the rock and on their steady breath:
– *Sherpa, search for our friend and I'll give you 100 dollars!*
They talk of a bird with an extreme facility for mimicry.
A bird which, they say, is called The Nohope,
the color of the jagged edge of a cliff.
And it only sings at the back of the ear's cave
when the air crystallizes
in that - insubstantial - blue.
The word of a sherpa who's had amputated
by frostbite
his fingers and toes
has always been very reliable.

Instantánea de una caída

El toldo de nieve arriba, y abajo el cuerpo de un escalador
de pierna fracturada.
Fue un sudaca que antes de morir tocó su flauta.
La montaña lo congela a uno, tomándole una foto
en una postura eterna.
Otros intentaron arrastrar aquel cadáver
lanzarlo por un risco.
Yo observé su rostro a través de un trozo de hielo:
las líneas del azar
se desmaterializaban en polvo blanco.
Al final, pude avizorar en sus pupilas estas secuencias:
el sudaca ascendía por la cara norte de la montaña
haciendo un dry-tooling,
una escalada libre y sin cuerdas.
Se veía tan pequeño que parecía avanzar
de pulgada en pulgada.
El viento no le permitía ver las banderas que ondeaban
en la antecumbre.
Luego se fue redireccionando.
Trató de comunicarse por radio,
mediante leves inflexiones de voz,
también lo hizo con movimientos.
[Se quedó mirando el aire / pero no encontró la rima].
Yo lo contemplaba con la imaginación absorta en otro asunto.
El olor de la muerte tiene una cierta realidad
que puede ser tasada en onzas o en gramos.

Hasta que cayó:
como el pichón de un petirrojo
de un nido inseguro.

No fue una tragedia: en poesía, tener fuerza de gravedad es más necesario que
tener la gracia divina. Es la atracción hacia la zona más negra de lo concreto.

Snapshot of a fall

The snow's awning above, below the body of a climber
with a broken leg.
It was a southerner who before dying played his flute.
The mountain freezes a man, taking a photo of him
in an eternal posture.
Others tried to drag that corpse,
to throw it over a cliff.
I observed his face through a chunk of ice;
the lines of fate
were dematerializing into white powder.
In the end, I was able to discern in his pupils these sequences:
the *Sudaca* was ascending by the north face of the mountain,
dry tooling,
climbing solo and without ropes.
He looked so small that he seemed to advance
inch by inch.
The wind didn't allow him to see the flags waving
on the subpeak.
Then he began to change direction.
He tried to communicate by radio
with slight inflections of his voice,
he also tried with gestures.
[He stared into the air/ but he didn't find the rhyme.]
I gazed at him with my imagination absorbed in another matter.
The odor of death has a certain reality
that can be valued in ounces or grams.

Until he fell,
like a robin fledgling
from an unsafe nest.

It was not a tragedy. In poetry, having the force of gravity is more necessary than
divine grace. It is the attraction toward the blackest zone of the concrete.

Urgente
(Un 11 de abril)

Muchos cuerpos piden ser reconstruidos: ¡Es un clamor!
Pero hay que seguir, hay que seguir, aunque el corazón
haga mutis
por sus recuerdos «imprecisos».
Los fantasmas se deprimen y se apartan.

Urgent
(One 11ᵗʰ of April)

Many bodies beg to be reconstructed. It's an outcry!
But we have to go on, we have to go on, even if the heart
drops out
because of its "imprecise" memories.
The ghosts become depressed and step aside.

Una lección

En el caserío Khabang
—luego de puentes que flotan sobre ríos de plata cruda—
hay un templo
y un Buddha
tallado en madera.
Los años mutilaron algunos dedos, incluso una mano,
y continúa con idéntica expresión sonriente:
Silenciemos el ruego
y pacifiquemos al que interroga.
Al principio, el Buddha de Khabang
era famoso por sus colores,
hasta que su piel se blanqueó mostrando
una cavidad más profunda.
La madera se abría en aristas rectas
y dejaba ver su fibra:
El hastío que conduce a la serenidad.

A lesson

In the Khabang hamlet
– after bridges floating over rivers of raw silver –
there's a temple
and a Buddha
carved in wood.
The years have amputated some fingers, even a hand,
and he still has the identical smiling expression.
Let us silence the plea
and pacify the one who queries.
At the start, the Buddha of Khabang
was famous for his colors,
until his skin whitened revealing
a deeper cavity.
The wood was splitting open in straight cracks
and showing its fiber:
The weariness that leads to serenity.

Mutilaciones

El tiempo mutiló la mano izquierda de la estatua de Meleagro,
pero... complacido y sereno, permanece
junto al enorme Jabalí de Calidón:
como a Álvaro Túniz, a quien encontraron de pie
con su misma postura de años
junto a su equipo de escalada.
Su cuerpo ya era de marfil, y el frío lo conservó para la eternidad.
El Apolo del patio del Belvedere, lastimosamente,
perdió el antebrazo derecho,
también su otra mano,
y sin embargo posa glorioso.
En igual posición se mantiene apoyado al pedernal
—con idénticas mutilaciones—
el cuerpo de Richard Olbrich.
O la escultura del muchacho romano del siglo III
    que corre sin cabeza.
Así le ocurrió al pequeño Alessio, que murió
al despeñarse por una grieta
y aún hoy lo podemos ver conservado
en un cubo rectangular de hielo.
O aquel torso romano, en mármol, sin extremidades:
¿no es igual a lo que resta de Tommaso Grimpolli
en el recodo de una ceñida galería con aparentes arcos y vidrieras?:
¿ustedes podrían imaginárselo?
O la cabeza del atleta
que fue esculpida sin ojos: ¿podrían preguntárselo?,
¿cómo es posible?...
Convengamos en algo:
Las mutilaciones acentúan el enigma de lo humano.

Mutilations

Time amputated the left hand of the statue of Meleager,
but... satisfied and serene, he is still erect
beside the enormous Boar of Calydon:
like Álvaro Túniz, whom they found standing
in the posture he'd held for years
beside his climbing kit.
His body was ivory now, and the cold had preserved him for
eternity.
The Apollo of the Cortile del Belvedere, regrettably,
lost his right forearm
and his other hand too,
and nevertheless his pose is glorious.
In the same position – with the same mutilations –
the body of Richard Olbrich
is still leaning against the rock.
Or the sculpture of the 3rd century Roman boy
       running without a head.
That's what happened to little Alessio, who died
on tumbling into a crevasse
and still today we can see him preserved
in a rectangular ice cube.
Or that Roman torso, marble, with no limbs:
isn't it the same as what's left of Tomaso Grimpolli
in the bend of a narrow gallery with what looks like arches
and display windows?:
can you imagine it?
Or the head of the athlete
carved without eyes: will you ask yourselves?
how can it be?...
Let's agree on one thing:
Mutilations accentuate the human enigma.

Demostración

Aquel sendero en la montaña,
no queriéndolo,
traduce perfectamente
el paso
de una sala a otra
en un museum.
Allí
los torsos de Laila Rosemberg y Amy Cubert:
el paño estucado de la nieve que los salvó del pus y lo podrido,
la grafía de los hielos eternos.
También todo se parece
al hojear de un lujoso catálogo:
imaginativos bodegones [tres latas de conservas
y unos lentes],
fotografías de performance
e instalaciones.

Demonstration

That trail up the mountain,
without meaning to,
translates perfectly
the passage
from one room to another
in a museum.
There
the torsos of Laila Rosemberg and Amy Cubert,
the stucco fabric of the snow that saved them from pus and rot,
the script of eternal ice.
Moreover it's all like leafing through
a glossy catalogue:
fanciful still-lifes [three tins of jam
and some dark glasses],
photos of performances
and installations.

Leo Feltrinelli

I   *Lo conocí sentado sobre el bajo antepecho*
de una losa granítica,
junto a un despeñadero vertical. La luz temprana del embudo
de un remolino de nieve
tragaba el aire gélido de la cara norte del Annapurna.
Hacia Leo Feltrinelli extendí mi brazo, y apoyado en la cáscara
del roquerío, le grité:
—Si te lanzas al abismo estarás en el camino de la gravedad
física. Persiste sobre la roca y serás perdonado
por la gracia de la nieve.
—No existe tal gracia (respondió). ¡Pero qué estupidez!
(Y continuó inmóvil, como la llama ordinaria de una
lámpara, en una habitación sin brisa alguna).

II *Compuso una canción titulada: Despreocupadas excursiones.*
Sin reparos, la Diosa le pidió los dedos de sus pies
bajo la escarcha del cielo. Se creía un experto en los caminos
que no se ven, una supuesta «geografía imaginaria»
que bordeaba el abismo de las rutas conocidas y el vacío
que debíamos superar, hasta saltar a lo más alto.
La vida de un escalador está llena de vertiginosas elipsis:
non sentiens, non dissentiens.
Yo creo que la montaña es una roca vibrante.
La noche que murió, lanzó con fuerza los dados
sobre el cantil de una mesa plegable para que oyéramos
su turno: pero siempre perdía, siempre perdía.

CODA
Una greguería nepalí:

Los ciegos miran las nubes
mientras comen.

Leo Feltrinelli

I   I met him sitting on the low parapet
    of a granite slab,
    above a vertical precipice. The early light in the funnel
    of a snow vortex
    swallowed the freezing air on the north face of Annapurna.
    Toward Leo Feltrinelli I stretched my arm and, leaning on
        the shell
    of the surrounding rock, I shouted at him:
    — If you throw yourself into the abyss you will be on the path of physical
    gravity. Persevere on the rock and you will be pardoned
    by the snow's grace.
    — There is no such grace (he answered). But how stupid!
    (And he remained immobile, like the ordinary flame of a
    lamp, in a room with no breeze.)

II He composed a song entitled: *Carefree excursions.*
    With no compunction, the Goddess asked him for his toes
    under the frosty sky. He believed himself an expert in paths
    not seen, a supposed "imaginary geography"
    that skirted the abyss of the known routes and the void
    we had to get over, then jumped to the highest point.
    The life of a climber is full of giddy ellipses:
    non sentiens, non dissentiens.
    I believe the mountain is a vibrating rock.
    The night he died, he threw the dice hard
    on the edge of a folding table so we would hear him play
    his turn: but he always lost, he always lost.

CODA
A Nepali couplet:

Blind men watch the clouds
while they eat.

Revelación inesperada

La voz de mi padre en el walkie-talkie.
Luego las voces de los amigos desde un bar en Hamburgo.
Piden que no me vaya sin tomar una copa
o besar al hijo que no conozco.
«Hay mucha estática».
El final será el coma hipotérmico.
Cuelgo del techo de un templo:
prácticamente en un nido de cuerdas
como si fuera un personaje de una foto de Nobuyoshi Araki.
Me falta dinero para llegar al Dios de Occidente…
Mientras…
el piadoso Vishnu susurró esta sentencia para mí:
los demonios lo empujaron desde un acantilado,
pero él cayó como una leve flor.

Unexpected revelation

My father's voice on the walkie-talkie.
Then the voices of friends from a bar in Hamburg.
They ask me not to go without having a drink
or kissing the son I don't know.
"There's a lot of static."
The end will be hypothermic coma.
I'm hanging from the roof of a temple,
practically in a nest of ropes
as if I was a figure in a photo by Nobuyoshi Araki.
I don't have the money to reach the God of the West...
In the mean time...
merciful Vishnu murmured this sentence for me:
the demons pushed him off a cliff,
but he fell as lightly as a flower.

Últimas convicciones

Un monje del convento recibe
una bufanda de lana de Cachemira
como regalo para el abad, mientras,
dos cabras entrechocan sus cabezas.
Otros monjes de doce y quince años
juegan al fútbol en el patio central
golpeando una lata de Coca-Cola.
También recortan esas latas para construirles bases a las velas
que luego ofrendan a Buddha.
Ciertamente, la montaña está atenta.
Una compañía de Travel & Trekking
asegura la posibilidad del ascenso
por un rastro de vísceras y dólares.
Los colmillos y calaveras que adornan el rostro de Buddha
no lograron inspirar respeto, ni ahuyentarnos:
seguimos llegando
en oleadas
de mil a mil.
Caminar sobre la nieve y tocar las rocas del Annapurna
tienen su precio.
En mi mente había filmado
por lo menos dos tráilers de esta aventura.
La carpa de fibra de nylon fue comprada
en una tienda que no existe en ninguna parte.
He ordenado sobre la nieve las carpas, marca Diamante,
triangulándolas
de forma religiosa en el campamento N°4
a 7.000 m de altura.
Desde ahí, hay una cordada de miserias hasta la cumbre.

Latest convictions

A monk in the monastery receives
a scarf of Cashmere wool
as a present for the abbot, while
two goats knock their heads together.
Other monks aged twelve and fifteen
play football in the central courtyard
kicking a Coca-Cola can.
They also trim those cans to use as holders for the candles
they will then offer to Buddha.
Certainly, the mountain is paying attention.
A Travel & Trekking company
ensures the ascent will be possible
by a trail of viscera and dollars.
The fangs and skulls adorning Buddha's face
weren't enough to inspire respect, or scare us off:
we kept on coming
in waves
thousands on thousands.
Walking on the snow and touching the rocks of Annapurna
has its price.
In my mind I had filmed
at least two trailers of this adventure.
The nylon fiber tent was bought
at a shop that exists nowhere.
I have set out the tents, Diamante brand, on the snow,
triangulating them
religiously at camp No.4
at 7,000 meters altitude,
From there, there's a rope of afflictions up to the summit.

En el descenso encontrarás la injuria
y la duda pajarística del Sinfé.
El Annapurna podría ser una pieza de un juego de lego
adquirida en la juguetería American Toy Store
de las Colinas de Bello Monte, en Caracas-Venezuela.
De esta manera llegamos a Dios con la escala del mercado,
rebotando hasta el arco de la consagración.

On the descent, you will discover the fraud
and doubt in the birdsong of the Nohope.
Annapurna could be a piece in a Lego game
bought at the American Toy Store
in Colinas de Bello Monte, Caracas-Venezuela.
Thus we come to God scaling the market,
bouncing right up to the ark of the covenant.

Declaración final de un funcionario

Yo estaba sobre el Annapurna y su peine negro y blanco
o quizás en mi oficina con los ojos congelados
en la pantalla del ordenador.
Huí a 10.000 a 20.000 m de altura
y me aparté hacia el estancado desierto del Paquistán:
o era mi rostro sobre papeles administrativos
y la tarde alcanzada en los informes.
Por los pasillos del Ministerio del Poder Popular para la Cultura
trotaban los rinocerontes de la anteguerra civil.
Todos sabemos lo bien que el diablo recita las escrituras.
Nada que hacer, nada que hacer
como no sea viajar con Google Earth.
Y si el salario se va por una zanja inmunda
juro no descender jamás del Annapurna:
—a las colinas del tedio
              torritremebundo—.
Amo la subjetividad de la copia, los estándares de luz
a distintas horas del día,
el cromatismo de un ordenador de buena marca, su resplandor
bien calibrado.
Para colmo (…) al salir del edificio no pude encender
mi amado Ford Thunderbird.
Y mis dos manos congeladas sobre su carrocería mansa
aguardaron el ocaso del trópico.

Final statement of a civil servant

I was on Annapurna and its black and white crest
or maybe in my office with my eyes frozen
on the computer screen.
I fled to 10,000, 20,000 meters altitude
and strayed toward the stagnant desert of Pakistan:
or it was my face over administrative documents
and the lateness of my reports.
Along the corridors of the Ministry of People's Power for Culture
trotted the rhinoceroses of impending civil war.
We all know how well the devil recites the scriptures.
Nothing I can do, nothing I can do,
except travel by Google Earth.
And if the salary runs away by a filthy ditch
I swear I will never descend from Annapurna
– to the hills of
                    terrible tedium–.
I love the subjectivity of the copy, the standards of light
at different hours of the day,
the chromatism of a computer of a good brand, its well
calibrated shine.
As a last straw (…) when I left the building I couldn't start
my beloved Ford Thunderbird.
And my two hands frozen on its placid body
awaited the tropical sunset.

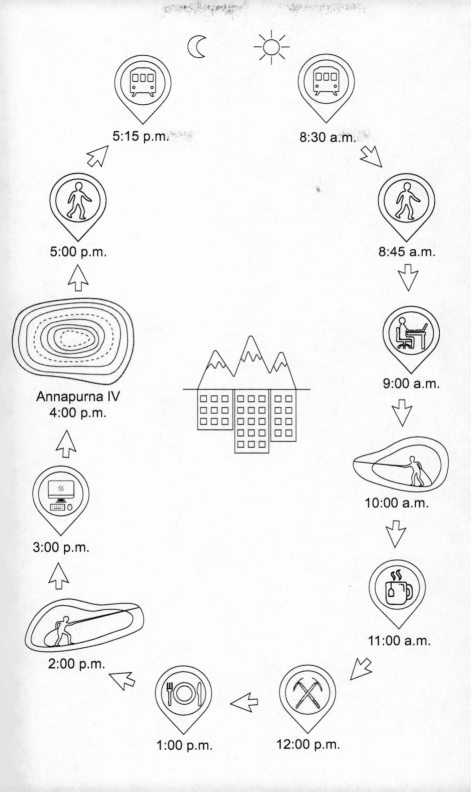

5:15 p.m.

8:30 a.m.

8:45 a.m.

9:00 a.m.

10:00 a.m.

11:00 a.m.

5:00 p.m.

Annapurna IV
4:00 p.m.

3:00 p.m.

2:00 p.m.

1:00 p.m.

12:00 p.m.

Canción final
soy un funcionario cuasi-metafísico

Siempre Drummond

Trabajo en el abismo,
trabajo en el vacío,
soy un funcionario
cuasi-metafísico.
Llevo mi vida a secas
en esta oficina
donde una enredadera
de malanga verde
es lo inalterable.
La señora María
—no hablo de la virgen—
dejó los vidrios como agua.
La bella dactilógrafa
y el mago del Kárdex
lamentan
su repentina cesantía,
su desventura implícita.
Infortunados, ellos,
aunque, con este sueldo
ya no se pueda vivir.
Al cruzar la puerta
supe que en mis huesos
estaba el silencio
de dos hojas blancas.
Conocí a Rosalía,
conocí a José,
a Rogelio Benavides:
el Jefe Interino
del Archivo Muerto.
Les mandé comunicaciones,
discutimos juntos

Final song
I am a quasi-metaphysical civil servant

Drummond again

I work in the abyss,
I work in the void,
I'm a quasi-metaphysical
civil servant.
I lead my stark life
in this office
where what doesn't alter
is a green
taro vine.
Señora María
– I don't mean the Virgin –
has left the windows like water.
The pretty typist
and the Kardex wizard
complain
of their sudden dismissal,
the bad luck it implies.
Unfortunate they are,
although with this salary
it's already impossible to live.
As I crossed the threshold
I knew that the silence
of two blank pages
was in my bones.
I met Rosalía,
I met José,
and Rogelio Benavides,
the Temporary Head
of the Dead Archive.
I sent them communications,
we discussed together

el presupuesto anual,
pero no recuerdo cómo eran.
Tal vez existieron,
no lo sé.
Mi vida se defiende
y los olvida.
Total, trabajamos «tanto»
para suprimir la casualidad.
Recuerdo un sacagrapas
con sus cuatro incisivos
afilados,
un edificio ministerial
como una montaña del Nepal,
el bolígrafo censurado
por el teléfono.
El idiota era cruel
y el energúmeno un verdugo.
Una tal Emily
preguntó:
—¿Quienes son los de abajo?
—Pues nosotros.
Se calma la memoria,
se aquieta mi afasia.
Como una mancha de café
así es el lunes,
como una mancha de café
así era el viernes.

the annual budget,
but I don't remember what they were like.
Maybe they existed,
I don't know.
My life defends itself
and forgets them.
All told, we worked "so hard"
to suppress chance.
I remember a staple remover
with its four sharp
incisors,
a ministry building
like a mountain in Nepal,
the ballpoint pen censured
by the telephone.
The idiot was cruel
and the maniac an executioner.
A girl called Emily
asked:
– *Who are the underdogs?*
– Well, us.
Memory calms down,
my aphasia subsides.
Like a coffee stain,
that's what Monday is,
like a coffee stain,
that's what Friday was.

mountain nepal himalaya nepal annapurna circuit trek annapurna m

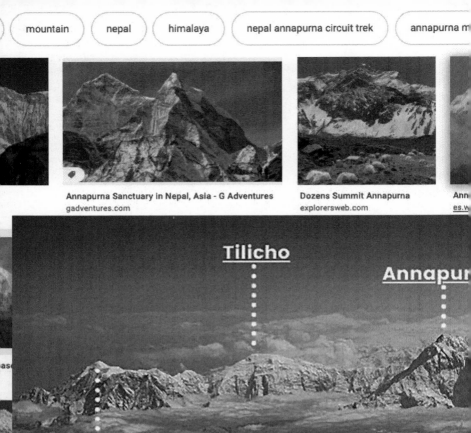

Tilicho

Annapur

Nilgiri North

Annapurna Sanctuary in Nepal, Asia - G Adventures
gadventures.com

Dozens Summit Annapurna
explorersweb.com

Ann
es.w

apurna Sanctuary – Adv...
enturesglobal.net

Annapurna Circuit - Wikipedia
en.wikipedia.org

Annapurna: the 10th Highest Mou
liveabout.com

nnapurna

annapurna sanctuary trek | annapurna south | maurice herzog | trail | climb

La maldición del Annapurna | Deportes | EL PAÍS
elpais.com

Annapurna circuit - Review of Annapurna Mou...
tripadvisor.com

Annapur...
switchbac

Gangapurna

Annapurna III

Annapurna II

Annapurna IV

purna South

on a

Before Hiking the Annapurna Circuit ...
nwanderer.com

Annapurna Nepal - mountain landscape oil ...
saatchiart.com

Annapurna V

Annapurna vs Everest Base...
nepalecoadventure.com

CONTENTS

🔍 All   📰 News   🖼 Images   📍 Maps   ▶ Videos   Settings   Tools

About 19,600,000 results (0.84 seconds)

en.wikipedia.org › wiki › Annapurna_Massif   ⋮

Annapurna Massif - Wikipedia

Annapurna is a massif in the Himalayas in north-central Nepal that includes one peak over 8,000 metres (26,247 ft), thirteen peaks over 7,000 metres (22,966 ft), ...

Parent peak: Cho Oyu   **Location:** Gandaki Zone, Nepal
Parent range: Himalayas   **Easiest route:** northwest face

Annapurna Circuit · Annapurna (goddess) · Annapurna (disambiguation) · Ueli Steck

---

People also ask   ⋮

Why is Annapurna so deadly?

What does Annapurna mean?

Is Annapurna the hardest mountain to climb?

What is the deadliest mountain in the world?

Fee

---

en.wikipedia.org › wiki › Annapurna_Circuit   ⋮

Annapurna Circuit - Wikipedia

The **Annapurna** Circuit is a trek within the mountain ranges of central Nepal. The total length of the route varies between 160–230 km (100-145 mi), depending ...

Trail difficulty: Difficult   **Length:** 131 kilometres (81 miles)
Elevation gain/loss: 10,107 m (33,159 ft) **Location:** Nepal

annapurna.pictures   ⋮

Annapurna Pictures

Annapurna Pictures is an American motion picture company founded by Megan Ellison in 2011. It specializes in film production, television production, video ...

www.muchbetteradventures.com › magazine › deadliest...   ⋮

Deadliest Mountain: The Story of Annapurna I

Sep 3, 2020 — **Annapurna** I is the tenth highest mountain in the world, at a not insignifica 8091m above sea level. It is part of the **Annapurna** massif in Nepal – ...

Annapurna

Massif in Nepal

4.5 ★★★★★ 253 Google reviews

Annapurna is a massif in the Himalayas in north-central Nepal that includes one peak over 8,000 metres, thirteen peaks over 7,000 metres, and sixteen more over 6,000 metres. Wikipedia

Elevation: 26,545′

Highest point: Annapurna I

Mountain range: Himalayas

Country: Nepal

Plan a trip

📷   Things to do

🛏   3-star hotel averaging $21

Passes: Thorong La

Mountains   View 4+ more

Annapurna I	Annapurna III	Annapurna II	Annapurna IV	Hiunchuli
26,545′	24,787′	26,040′		21,132′

ANNAPURNA. THE EMPIRICAL MOUNTAIN
FABLES OF A QUASI-METAPHYSICAL CIVIL SERVANT | IGOR BARRETO

Made in Miami Beach ~ Printing as needed

◊◊◊

2021

Made in the USA
Columbia, SC
27 September 2023

23500682R10062